Pet Rats And Mice Handbook

Alkeith O Jackson

Copyright Notice

Disclaimer and Terms of Use

First Printing, 2014

ISBN-13: 978-1500762605

PET RATS AND MICE HANDBOOK

HOUSING - FEEDING AND CARE

CONTENTS

PET RATS AND MICE

White mice and white rats are often kept as pets, and are popular to have as pets. They are very tame and are usually gentle and affectionate, they are as interesting and desirable as many other tame animals.

Many generations of breeding have produced the numerous varieties of white, piebald, and tortoise-shell mice and rats, but their natural character has not changed.

They are not the most beautiful animals, for regardless of color or docility they always look like rats, and the natural aversion of many people to these animals cannot be overcome. The common brown or black house rat or the ordinary little brown mouse can be tamed and domesticated and, as a rule, they are just as intelligent as the fancy varieties, and yet few people would care for these animals as pets.

Tame rats and mice may be taught a number of tricks.

Of the two I think the mice are preferable to the rats. They are cleaner in habits and require less room and are, as a rule, more docile. Rats are always treacherous and are likely to bite their owner without warning, and the wounds inflicted by their teeth are always dangerous.

Rats, moreover, are well-known carriers of disease, and where there is any contagious disease it is likely to be transmitted by rats or mice. Even if tame rats are kept in cages and isolated some wild rat is likely to carry disease to them, and in places where bubonic plague or cholera is epidemic, rats are now known to spread these terrible diseases from place to place.

HOUSING, CARE AND FEEDING

Rats and mice are easily kept and do not require a great deal of care. Small wire cages with a nest basket or compartment are suitable for these creatures, but the floor tray should be easy of access and should be cleaned and scrubbed daily.

The sleeping compartment should be filled with soft rags, cotton, or tow, which the animals will tear up and form into a nest. Water should always be provided, and the food should be given in small dishes and only enough to satisfy the rats or mice should be fed at one time, although a dish of dry corn, wheat, or small nuts may be kept in the cage at all times for the animals to nibble at between meals.

Rats and mice delight in exercise, and branches and perches should be provided as well as swings. Wheels are often placed in the cages for rats and mice, and the animals often whirl around and around in these contrivances. They are not desirable, however, for the long tails of the rodents often become injured or broken in the wheels. Swings will afford all the exercise required, and even branches or perches will give the pets ample opportunities to run and scamper about.

Tame rats and mice will eat almost anything and everything just the same as wild rats or mice, but' they should not be given everything they will eat. Dry bread crusts, grain, corn, green food, vegetables, and fruit should be their diet, and in warm weather corn and nuts should be fed sparingly.

Meat should never be given or your pets will become vicious and devour one another. Insects may, however, be given from time to time, and nuts, especially hickory-nuts and filberts, may be fed freely in winter-time and sparingly in summer.

A good-sized piece of wood, preferably a piece of green wood with the bark on, should be left in the cage at all times for the animals to gnaw. If the rats do not have something to gnaw on their teeth will grow abnormally long and will eventually kill them.

Clean sawdust sprinkled with disinfectant should be spread over the tray of the cage. Care should be taken in using a disinfectant, as many of these substances are very poisonous to animals. Oil of eucalyptus is the safest and best compound.

This should be diluted with water—about one teaspoonful of the oil to a cup of water—and sprinkled on the sawdust and all portions of the cage with an atomizer. When the mother rat or mouse has young the male should be taken away and placed in another cage, as otherwise he will kill or devour his young family. It is claimed by some that this is abnormal, and that if fed sufficiently the male will not devour the young. This is true in the case of many animals, but my experience is that rats and mice will become cannibals even when given all the good food they will eat.

Do not overfeed; give just as much as they will eat at one time and no more, and if you find any food remaining after an hour or two, reduce the next meal accordingly. Do not feed soft, mushy, or sloppy foods; nature gave rodents teeth for gnawing, and unless they are used for the purpose intended the animals will become sickly and their teeth will become too long.

There are numerous breeds or varieties of tame rats and mice, but each belongs to one of the two species, and has been produced from wild brown forms by selecting and breeding. Pure white animals with pink eyes are the commonest variety.

Others are white with brown or black spots, while others are "tortoiseshell," or have several colors combined. Still other varieties are pale-gray, others black with white markings, and others yellow or orange.

The so-called "waltzing mice" are merely animals with a brain disease which causes them to run in circles or in an erratic manner. They were originally produced in Japan and may be bred easily in confinement. They are amusing, but to many persons their affliction seems more pitiful than interesting.

WILD RATS AND MICE

The commonest of all rats and mice are the brown animals. These are foreigners and were introduced from Europe with the earliest settlers. The rarer Black Rat is also European but is so much weaker and less pugnacious than the brown rats that in most places it has been exterminated by them.

The common brown rats and mice are a nuisance to most people, while others find them attractive. Their habits are not the same as the white mice and white rats. Many people are averse to any rat or mouse, and have quite overlooked the fact that lots of species found wild are very handsome and attractive.

Some of the wild wood and field mice and rats are exceedingly graceful in form, beautiful in color, and interesting in their habits. The common White-Footed Mouse, known also as the Deer-Mouse, Wood-Mouse, or Field-Mouse, is a very lovely and lovable creature. In color this dainty fellow is warm fawn, reddish-buff, or even golden, with a darker back and snow-white feet, legs, and lower parts. The ears are large, the eyes big and soft, and the tail quite thickly clothed with hair.

Another very pretty species is the Harvest-Mouse, a dainty little creature less than 2 inches in length, with a prehensile tail, which it uses much in the manner of an opossum or monkey.

These pretty creatures build nests in grass or among grain or take possession of an old bird's nest. They are easily tamed and become very affectionate and have very little of the objectionable mouse-like odor.

Among the larger rats there are also many attractive wild species which make far more desirable pets than the tame white variety. The Wood-Rat of the South and West is a beautiful species, with a well-furred tail. This animal is bright tawny or golden-yellow above, with pure white breast, throat, feet, and belly, and has very soft, large eyes.

The wood-rats live in trees and make large, bulky nests. They are as lively and attractive as squirrels, and run and jump from tree to tree with the utmost facility. In many places they are considered excellent eating, their flesh being as white and well flavored as that of a rabbit or squirrel.

OTHER RAT-LIKE CREATURES

Many animals related to rats and mice have the power of jumping for long distances, and have the hind feet and legs wonderfully developed so that they resemble miniature kangaroos in appearance and habits.

Jerboas

The common jerboas of Africa have large ears, small front feet, and enormous hind feet, and travel almost entirely by hops and skips, using their tufted tail as a fifth leg.

They are interesting, pretty creatures and easily domesticated. We do not need to look to the Old World for representatives of these kangaroo-like mice, however. In the United States we have several wild species, the commonest being the Jumping Mouse, which is found from the Atlantic coast to the Pacific, as far north as New England and Canada. This odd mouse has very powerful hind feet and a long tail, and when alarmed makes off with great leaps of 8 or lo feet at a bound.

Ordinarily, however, the little fellow moves about on all fours like ordinary mice. The Jumping Mouse lives mainly in the woods and sleeps and breeds in cozy grass nests in hollow trees or in burrows in the earth. It is easily tamed and makes an interesting pet.

The Pocket-Mouse

A still more remarkable species is the Pocket-Mouse of the Southwestern States. This remarkable animal is fawn-colored above and white below, with white feet and a white stripe on the hips.

The fur is as fine and soft as silk, and the eyes are very large and lustrous. The head is abnormally large—or the body abnormally small—and this with the enormous hind legs and diminutive front feet and long, tufted tail gives the tiny creature a very droll and unusual appearance. This animal is very easily tamed and becomes exceedingly affectionate.

Unfortunately, he is nocturnal in habits and spends a good deal of his time sleeping during the day. If, however, he is fed in the daytime and food is not left in his cage at night he will very soon learn to sleep at night and keep awake in the day like ordinary animals.

The true Kangaroo Rats of Australia are not rats at all but marsupials, and are related to the kangaroos. They are about as large as rabbits and make very attractive and interesting pets.

They feed mainly on roots and vegetables and do not gnaw like true rats. Various other creatures related to the rats are found in the United States, among them being the odd Pouched Gophers, or Pocket-Rats, curious animals with short tails, strong, long-toed front feet, and remarkably powerful teeth.

These animals grow to large size—sometimes a foot in length. Their cheeks are provided with enormous pouches in which they carry a supply of food to their burrows.

As they are always hungry and are continually burrowing about and devouring roots, they prove very destructive to vegetation in many places. In some parts of the West and Southwest they are a serious pest, and thousands of them are killed yearly by the farmers. Although so destructive, they have interesting ways and may be kept in captivity.

The Hamster

Somewhat similar in habits to the Pouched Gophers is the hamster of Europe and Asia. This animal is about lo inches long, with a short tail. The color is rich yellowish or tawny-brown, with black, yellow, and red markings on the head and with the lower parts black.

The coloration is very striking, and the fur of the animal is used a great deal for lining coats and ladies' wraps. The hamster builds roomy, underground galleries and in these stores great quantities of grain, roots, and other food. Like our common woodchuck, the hamster sleeps through the winter and wakes in the spring with a healthy appetite, which it at once satisfies on the store of provisions it has so wisely provided. Although irritable and pugnacious when wild, yet the hamster is easily tamed and does well in confinement.

The Lemming

The remarkable lemmings of the northern portions of Europe, Asia, and America are also related to rats and mice but are very different in appearance. They are quite small—only 5 or 6 inches in length—but they are so exceedingly numerous at times as to overrun the entire country and prove a menace to everything in their path.

When migrating or when travelling from the mountains to the lowlands, the lemmings at times appear in vast multitudes. They proceed straight on their course, regardless of rivers, lakes, or other barriers.

They are insensible to danger and invade houses and towns, devouring everything edible which they find, and passing in an irresistible army until they reach the sea.

On their marches thousands are killed by birds of prey, animals, and men, but they are so numerous that there seems to be but little diminution in their numbers. Such tidal waves of animals only occur occasionally and are due either to an abnormal increase in the numbers of the animals or a scarcity of food in their native haunts or to both causes combined.

The great numbers of the animals killed on the march decreases the hordes until the balance of nature is re-established, and the lemmings retire to oblivion for several years. In color the lemmings are dappled with chestnut, black, gray, and buff, with a white collar, tail, and feet.

In some species the coat becomes entirely white in winter. The fur is dense, soft, and silky and reaches well over the feet and toes. The lemmings, being arctic animals, are very hardy. They feed upon herbage, grains, roots, and insects, and are very easily kept in captivity. They soon become tame and gentle and make interesting and desirable little pets.

Any variety of the wild mouse may be easily captured in box traps or caught in their nests, and any boy who lives in the country or near woods and fields can obtain interesting pets in this way. After you have kept some of the cunning and really pretty wild mice or wood-rats you will wonder why anyone ever keeps the uninteresting and commonplace ones.

Hamster

Siberian Brown Lemming

Wild Rat

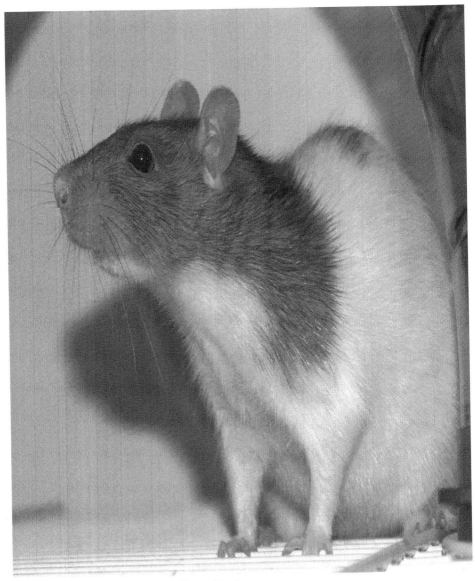

Pet Rat

Alkeith O Jackson